DECK OF DEEDS

DECK

RODRIGO

OF

TOSCANO

DEEDS

Counterpath
Denver
2012

Counterpath
Denver, Colorado
www.counterpathpress.org

Library of Congress Cataloging in Publication Data

Toscano, Rodrigo.
    Deck of deeds / Rodrigo Toscano.
      p.   cm.
    ISBN 978-1-933996-31-8 (pbk. : alk. paper)
    I. Title.
PS3570.O739D43   2012
811'.54—dc23
                          2011052749

Life consists not in holding good cards
but in playing those you hold well.
—JOSH BILLINGS

The price of anything is the amount of
life you exchange for it.
— ANTON CHEKHOV

What could be more convincing than
the gesture of laying one's cards face
up on the table?
—JACQUES LACAN

LOS EXPLORADORES

Last summer, while on their first gulf-wide helicopter tour, they learned how to increase their inner-narrating capacities with a titanium-coated needle. They prefer to stoke it in small basements of large soccer stadiums south of the equator in case they encounter too much cerebrospinal spillage, or regulation. Their favorite fantasy is that they're successful motivational vocabularists for hire to a half dozen oil executives from Russia on a visit to New York who install an indecipherable ethicalism into their brains, one by one.

Last week, while still twisted on dichlorobenzidine after a night of doctoring EPA reports, they licked the sweet crude slime from a 200-meter drill bit before going in for a final, deep plunge. Just as they were about to induce a frontal cranial orgasm for the stockholder's executive board, they looked into their faces in a reflective aluminum hotel bar counter-plating in Houston. When they saw how hot their mouths looked, smeared with oil, spit, and tar gas residue, they gazed into their own eyes and whispered, "We're such . . . sluts."

LOS SALVADOS

Last month, a Middle Eastern creed (much older than theirs) they met at a "Mysteries of Faith" convention in Raleigh, North Carolina, fed them their own arteryworks in the privacy of their hotel rooms. Together, they sorted white platelet from red platelet then strained the remains into a tin-glazed porcelain chamber pot. They slow-drip fed from the substance for hours. The much older creed then stuffed their apocalyptic pronouncements back into their mouths. While on their backs, goat legs of Beelzebub clamped together, the much older creed transmuted their "Practicalities of Providence" into a translucent blue liquid. After adding a dollop of its black-green colored warring bile into the chamber pot, the creed took out the complimentary holy books from their lamp drawers and brushed them against their nostrils. Like little animals, they sniffed them, and stuck their tongues out.

EL BEBE

All three presidential candidates have ample, basalt granite tempo-ral lobes, including the baby. His lobes are especially "crackly"— they flake at even 10 MHz. His closest advisor, the English lan-guage, lasers his lobes with bestseller lists until he almost passes out. He's learned to need it, require it, love it—brutally so—at least once a month. He submits to at least one bestseller three weeks before leaving on cross-country tours so that the fracturing has time to heal, as he has a Squishy Head VP nominee who disap-proves of the crackled look. Sometimes this violence scares the baby, but he feels very calm and in command afterward.

LA EXPERTA

Her distal phalanges grew, year by year. She learned how to tuck them into ever-silkier and ever-daintier gloves. Her brow ridges swelled, year by year. She learned how to shape them into meal-sized protrusions that make mouths water. Her stock derivatives portfolio lips split open, year by year. She learned how to ride mechanical horses in DC, frontwards and backwardss. She learned how to swing her legs up clear over the banister in her home state's municipal chamber. She learned how to grip at collars while swinging upside-down suspended on a rubber cord as wooden nickels fell out of her pockets.

She knows what America needs. She's out to get it—today. *Yay*!

EL PROFE

Five things his students don't know about him:

He lets his pubes grow out while on sabbatical.

He frequently employs aides for lecturing: carisoprodol, glutethimide, gamma-hydroxybutyrate.

He has a department head who enjoys "loaning him" to visiting fellowships (he enjoys *her* enjoyment).

He lets any "experimental" poet with at least three publications post their twitters in all his portals.

He keeps a trusty supply of Tetracycline in his office drawer.

EL SIRVIENTE

It's been a busy week for the public servant.

On Monday, he planned for the Three Gorges presidential tour of China in the spring.

On Tuesday, he lowered the black curtains on the International Labor Organization's "Respiratory Diseases" yearly report and let Canada's visiting Tar Sands rep take an impromptu whizz in the Oval Office.

On Wednesday, he fired an "over sensitive" staffer after a department meeting.

On Thursday, he hired a staffer he met at a Lithium Industries mixer.

On Friday, in the morning, he agreed to lowering minimum standard requirements for Hazardous Waste cleanup while visiting Mexico; later that day, he fired an "over inquisitive" staffer—in an elevator—before a meeting; in the evening, he promoted the Lithium Industries staffer—by e-mail.

On Saturday, he promised to limit labor union "influence" at the Commerce Club in Boston; he then flew back to DC, laid a little turd in behind a lavish wall curtain in the West Wing, and then walked over to the East Wing to direct his staff to wring out as much "working language" as can be had from the word *freedom*; finally, he ended up at the Dominican Republic's embassy, fighting for a Free Trade Zone late into the night.

Busy week for the public servant.

EL COMERCIANTE

Here to inform you that your fetus is into providing weapons to other fetuses at select places around the world. It picked up the taste for this trade two months ago while you were all on vacation in Florida. That "nice fetus from Oregon" who taught your fetus how to properly synthesize proteins in macrophage cell membranes, remember? By the fourth day they were filling invoices for M1A2 Abrams Tank spare parts.

On the fifth day, your fetus reverently tumbled onto its belly facing the center of the earth, and flapped its proto-real lips at it for about thirty minutes.

What does your fetus like about it (the center of the Earth, that is)? Like you, it loves the gritty mineral-like taste of deep-buried dirt thrown into its proto-real face. It also loves volcano vapors searing the skin off of its proto-real fanny while plunging its proto-real vestigial tail into the clear aquamarine waters of—birthdom.

How many fetuses total has it sold weapons to? Just four hundred thousand. But it's hooked. Your fetus foresees a lifetime of weapons sales across the globe. It's got a gold ring on its belly now too (or head, hard to say).

LOS INGENIEROS

The slightest speck of sulfur acid speckled onto the primary fracking tanks' gelatinous ethanol surface at the entrance to the central burner, and it'll be ready to spawn a substance which will harden into a very similar grade of carbon-derivative solids containing a very voluble, catalytic little society.

EL EDIFICIO

Bitch. No other word best describes this office tower in an overall way. Bitch to bridges, bitch to canals, freeways—to recreational and commerce purposes alike. It was most likely an "accident" inspiration, unplanned, unjustified, but this is *its* existence now.

It gussies up in blue and red lights for the night, and when it weaves and wavers in the eyes of its subjects, its hallucinatory power pervades the space wherever it happens to be (this building is ambulatory). Both its subjects and subjects' subjects feel the urge to drop to their knees to get a near-vertical view of its majesty. Its pulsing busy lobby counts for any other three pulsing busy lobbies put together in any pulsing busy global lobby.

Its Structural Adjustment muscle can grip the biggest of debtor nations—milk them clean of futures. It does just that. It's got "options."

EL LIBRITO

Not only did the orbital radius of Jupiter get thrown off by 24 million miles as a beam of light first struck his new book of retro-modernist aesthetics, but a far-off star expired at that very moment.

Perfection like it was never before seen, nor ever since. Nay, Ambition itself snuck off to a shy corner of Life out of fear of being overshadowed forever by this book.

There are books, and then there's *this* book. Of man born? Yes. By man induced? Yes. Impossible to believe, but yes—from *both*, equally.

The Stellar Globular Clusters in Virgo demand that this book be consumed from cover to cover.

The Stellar Globular Clusters in Virgo also demand that every breath of it be captured and gifted back to it as ecstatic continuous pleasure.

LA PALABRITA

Your gut feeling was right. The word, Liberty, didn't actually go visit an old friend from the French Revolution last month. It's having a fling—with two silver-haired MP's from the Netherlands. It met them on a train during its trip through Europe last year. They got really drunk on ready-made anti-immigrant rhetoric, and stumbled into Frankfurt station in Germany. The three went monopoly media hopping, and ended up amnesiating (or, amnesiacking) *out*—in a booming techno club. The three woke up tangled in each other's lexical matrices in a toilet bowl. And now, here's Liberty, in another toilet bowl, in Manhattan, about to announce its candidate's candidacy while its candidate clamps its candidacy in its candidate's candidacy.

LOS CULTOS

Besides learning archeo-Babylonian, studying alchemy, and volunteering at a Hippopotamus Cancer Center, she's learned to love poetry. She prefers it to "regular culture" almost every time now. While on all fours, the Hippopotamus is very strong, but not entirely able to back her up on the National Poetry Foundation website. Her trust fund helps though, especially for the breathing part. *Who* does she practice breathing with? Her landlord. Relax. She's saving *tons* of cultural capital. She's her own landlord. She's busy negotiating a complex, new world. *Who* did she learn these skills from? Your derivative class-erasing alibis. They intimated this specialized knowledge to her sometime back. And now, *she* is about to intimate it to *her* derivative class-erasing alibis.

EL DIABLITO

"Diablito," they affectionately call him at Family of Labor reunions. He doesn't look like a diablito at all really; he looks more like a sleek young barracuda. However you cut it, he's 100% primate.

Over the last six months, he's developed a strong attraction to scrawny, even slightly decomposed legislation, legislation "clearly" below his "game."

It happened at a corny Marti Gras event in his medium-sized job-depressed town—everyone was in masks. Sum of it is, at around 3:00 a.m., he found himself gagging on a Wall Street-Labor Cooperation bill that stretched his mouth in all directions, seriously challenging his gag reflex.

He—*enjoyed* it. "Diablito"—likes'em *fully earmarked* now.

LOS TERRESTRIALES

It's a very exclusive club. Only one out of every couple hundred Andromedans who audition ever get to go on. "Go on" at this club means getting stress-tested in the latest alien casing designs and posing for seated academics. Every academic gets its own Andromedan for two hours—in a private lab. Almost no base code is ever exchanged. The room's lasers of various spectrums and pulse rates are controlled by them, so is the dispensation of deuterium fluoride compounds and mixtures. They are not allowed to touch the Andromedans or to proposition them in any way. They are, however, in full command of what they're *meaning* to say at any given time.

This fuselage covering in particular conforms to the molecular bonding interpretive frame that one of its regulars has it display. They're an older couple, in their early 60's. Their obsessive crush on this Andromedan has cost them over $10,000 in club passes and "extras" over the last six years.

Their fantasy (of which the Andromedan is only murkily aware) is that it's been scanning phenomena rich in the rubidium of their own logarithmically calculated eventual decay of that element. It brings them to an agitated electrons jump-point thinking of this Andromedan's avant-garde, cadmium-corseted waste pressurizing a singular long ingot of rubidium into its lower propellant fuel chamber. The spiraling super-heated conception is about to be expelled into an oxygen-rich atmosphere—at any moment.

The Andromedan believes they have an avant-garde, cadmium-corset fetish, pure and simple, so it double-flash welds every single rivet, very precisely, till they're all flush, till all of the encasement specs are "realized," till the Andromedan can barely breathe.

The Andromedan's smile is as digitally scrambled sweet as you've always known it to be, plus, it always did like to play "inter-galactic artist," right?

LA EXPERIMENTALISTA

Anywhere and *everywhere*, that's her thing now, to *work it—* whenever.

Here she is in the alley crouched next to the apartment complex dumpster, the same place she experimented with *splork* poetry last summer. Her older cousin passed the genre down to her. She keeps a copy of *Leopard Skin Village* tucked away in a white cosmetic bag in her purse. She never washes it really. Once in a while she might slip the book into her mouth and lick it clean. Just yesterday, she put it in her mother's porcelain glass case teacup cabinet, to see what if felt like. She found it strangely pleasurable. She's decided to relocate it again this weekend in the storage locker where her dad keeps eight retired 250 MHz/100MB Dell desktop towers. *Yes*, she's made a duplicate key and thus has *access* to the storage locker. The darkness and coolness of the place makes her extra introspective. Also, in those conditions, she's able to say things out loud she might not otherwise: "I want Penguin Books to publish me"; "I want a hard, red & black, glossy cover to add extra significance to it."

LA LICENCIADA

Her ethics have gotten much denser, more padded since she wrote her dissertation, "Agentic Arenas of Pilfering (A New Genre)" at Swarthmore. Her philosophical underpinnings now smother each other in almost every logical position, snuggling her puckered historical-materialist soft spot.

The novelist's scene she now frequents caters to aspirants much older than herself. Her new job requires a certain kind of attire. She would surprise you by her skill at handling an absinthe list. Even her way of carpet bombing the comments section of *Boston Review On-Line* has gotten more sophisticated: a shiny tin case with neatly stacked cue cards, placed smartly inside her white latex trench coat houses the youth-impulsive utterances.

She's got two reverse-aging guy novelists who work for the emerging genre. Each one knows about the other; they accept the situation. They share panels with her at different conferences. She never reveals what she does to their work in *real* critical theory circles to either of them. She does have several genres off to herself though.

Lately, on those genre-free nights, she's been looking at quality on-line repurpositive art. It's crystallizing in her mind that all of her switches are flipped on by reverse-aging women who unabashedly exude para-inhibitory repurpositive critical art power. Her fantasy is to submit a decades labored-over source text to one of them, and to evanish therein thereafter henceforth thereby.

She's not sure how much evanishment she wants, but she suspects *a lot*.

EL SURFEADOR

You've feared this. And now here it is. Your hours of surfing self-publishing sites have turned this up. From the pdf's date, it seems it was created on March 19, 2011, at 4:00 a.m. That day, two (of the four) of your split personalities went to war against Saudi Arabia and Israel at the same time; oil painting vs. water painting—"all you need to know," kept the other two busy.

That's *your* laptop cam. That's also its manufacturer's (your employer's) signature trace-bit kernel in your I.D. pic's file extension. And yes, that twitch in your third eye is very disturbing.

EL ORGANISMO

At an early stage, this Sclerocephalus learned that it could make itself feel super good by straddling its capellini-like legs and gnawing hard on the edge of its "parent" volcanic rock's micro-cratering.

A few million years later, it discovered that by rubbing a rain-slick banana leaf repeatedly across its primate groin for one eighth of one degree quarter turns of the sun's path, that the pleasant sensation lasted for two sixths of one half eighth turn of the sun's path.

A few hundred million years after that, it stuck a large turkey feather into a vial containing burnt bone grinds mixed with pitch. It learned that by artfully brushing the feather along a pressed sheet of wood pulp rendering quantities of goods (including slaves), The Empire expanded to new proportions, also becoming more amenable to a certain one god's oneness.

At age two billion and one (while mom was visiting on winter break) he accidently left open the folder titled "new calculations" (which was nested into the folder "equations & formulas") while he was taking a shower. Mom happened to stroll into his bedroom, and counted twelve prostatic plexus vein boric acid self-infusion videos, seven anterior pudenal arterial ablation high-res pics, and five full-length films of him sensually posing in Late American Empire formal wear in different promote-me positions. When the shower faucet was suddenly shut off, mom briskly closed the video program before slinking out of the room.

The two later had a relaxed and enjoyable lunch at the campus vegan collective.

LA SOLDADA

Her new beau (who's 154 years her senior) snapped this pic of her in full desert gear before attending their first "soft" annexationists open water-boarding party. As the fateful day grew nearer, her belly clenched itself into knots, apprehensive by the unknown that lay ahead.

Shortly after they arrived (after removing the tarp from the new transport vehicle, revealing the pricey bulletproof glass), two battalion commanders invited her to engage an enemy combatant over a long oval glass table. The old *perruque* (whatever that means) got rather nervous, but also extremely perruque'd as she bent her eager face over the glass to get her very first taste of the enemy.

Within ten minutes she was relating the experience excitedly to a U.N. type by the mess hall, fast-assembling her M-15 wearing a blindfold and nervously gestimating her total clip count. She would occasionally glance back at her "grey-eyed man of destiny" from across the yard with a glaze in her eyes, but for the most part, she was locked into the coalitional partner.

Suddenly, the U.N type's Chinese-made rocket launcher pointed straight at her M-15; her head dipped down in a near-comatose apprehension of the situation. She then slowly raised her eyes to the perruque (alias William Walker) with a shy but determined look. A slight smile came over her face as the U.N. corporal slowly hoisted her onto the helicopter's lift chair. Her beau's peanut-sized heart pounded out of his chest, awaking in his soul a new awareness of nation-love as the two disappeared into the sky above.

She emerged nine years and a half later, her face with a distinct pink grapefruit hue of having been thoroughly re-juiced at the International Tribunal at The Hague. She also had dozens of kiwi skin scratches on her diplomatic resume.

"Pumpkin" (as she still prefers to be called by you) grew up on her older brother's "hidden" browser links, her favorite site being "abductmylittleimperialistsis.com"

EL AMBICIOSO

"Dear Sis,

I loved that last talk we had, when we decided to not feel inhibited anymore when talking about exploiting Mexicans. *So . . .*

Here's me backstage hiring a Mexican at the Indie Restaurant Festival in Little Rock. He took this pic of the two of us just as it got started. His dish-cleaning turnover rate was one the best I've ever witnessed, fast as the headwaters log ride at Knott's Berry Farm, but very affordable. I was waiting for him to feed a blueberry muffin into my mouth when . . . *oops*—wrong storyline . . . alright, when he flashed a National Labor Relations Act flash card in my face, and sang "solidaridad para siempre" into my ears.

I was really entrepreneurially pumped, so I had the card framed that very evening. It was laminated with a holographic image of Jimmy Hoffa when viewed at an angle. Made me think whoever gave it to him was "prepped" for this kind of thing. Maybe this is how these people get their freak on—I don't know. I had never framed a laborer's rights under the U.S. Constitution ever before (have you?). I liked it! He punched me in the face just as I was uploading a clip of it on YouTube. We quickly composed ourselves, and exchanged digits. He said he would send me our original festival meeting pic during tomorrow's May Day rally. He did! I have to admit, I was really impacted by this quickie kind of historical update, especially the plastic surgery stuff.

C u at the end of the first quarter report meeting,

Big Bro"

LOS FREGONES

What's that look on their faces mean? They're *fregnated*. Your moon traffic controller buddy turned them on to it about a month ago.

They were Earth gazing from inside the Rest & Relaxation module, wearing those chromium dioxide meshed layerings that make you feel so *pent up* whenever they wear them. Your buddy's main task that day was to talk to them about new travel procedures (that was the very day you two teed up at Armstrong's Super 18 Challenge, the day you two tag-team double-spec'd the operator-in-training working the buggy ammonium oxide tanks).

When they heard the thump-thump on the module's underside, they engaged the service hydraulics, and let him in through the rear flap vent. Just like you trained them to—to be good moonscape artists (as well as hosts), they (all twenty of them) immediately coalesced around the central cooling unit and decanistered your cask of *Fregnator Ten Hop Triple I.P.A.*

The conversations that ensued are nearly impossible to re-create: alternate landing coordinates, de-freezing ion-bonded surfaces, "terminal" vs. "terminal-terminal" approaches to touch-down points—etc., all ending in a throat-catching moment of silence. Before they knew what hit them, they found themselves piling into four buggies, furiously riding off into the Mare Tranquillitatis.

They well knew your buddy would block their joyride, and that, by having inadequate frontal radar protection, they were risking it. They couldn't stop. They *wouldn't* stop. Once they'd committed to jamming his signal breaker so that their projected paths went straight past his path re-scrambler, they sped up, bouncing on the buggies that much harder.

You should know that this was their fourth foiled joyride to the dark side of the moon (some of them of them have, however, applied for some small-scale explorative missions to Mars—at least two).

So what steps were taken to retrain these moonscape artists that fregnated themselves? Let's just say, not *exactly* addressed in the Moon Governing Manual.

EL ALUMNO

"Worker behavior-based accident." That's the phrase his intriguing new older friend likes him to rhapsodize on. And that's just what this very serious young corporate industrial hygienist gives him. And lots of it.

He met him six months ago at an airport bar during a layover on the way back from an Abba comeback concert tour in Orange, California. Never in a million years could he have imagined getting entangled into a toxic chemical reaction chain with another alumni from MIT.

It happens mainly on the mesas of Ciudad Juárez, in half kilometer-wide lithium sulfur tubs. The young hygienist enjoys the challenge of allegorizing the letting loose of a whole day's worth of run-off into the neighborhoods in the valley below, and his intriguing new friend is relieved by the redirected torrent of guilt, shame, and depression that engulfs somebody else's every sensation.

The only other alumni who know about these lucrative enterprises are his intriguing new friend's two other friends (brothers) who've got a thing for Tea Bags dunked in brackish waters. *Party party party.*

EL BARQUITO

It doesn't belch smoke nor set to harbor anymore. It hardly even ever "docks," properly speaking. Choppy swells, it's not the least bit tempted by. Hauling planes on its back, it's left behind too. All-night engagements with sneaky underwater things—are a thing of the past. It's also given up on incessant radar frequency replicating habits. Its long-standing fixation with collecting seaworthy skinny men in its hull—has been overcome. It also doesn't send international warning signals to strangers anymore—ever.

Its lukewarm sponsors increasingly scoff at this daily performance, which involves it "wearing" and "being true" to what it calls its "conceptual-national nipple-clamp." But the more *biting* truth is that even its true friends in Congress (all two) are crazily jealous because it has so clearly mastered the art of total control over foreign diplomats at U.N. parties. Virtually any diplomat in the room could very well become *its*—exclusively curious about "American Culture," or not.

In this death match between "patriotic monument" and "world heritage site," it doesn't care which side "wins" really, as it *always*

ends up administering the most enthusiastic, deeply transforma-
tive junk-time of any industrial product it knows.

In other words, it's the *ultimate* slut—"the exhibit you want."

EL DEDICADO

He can't quite decide on which $9 an hour job to dedicate his life to. He often thinks maybe he should have waited a year or two, occupied a country or two, before enrolling in the Iowa Writer's Workshop, maybe scatter falafel flour with the tip of his own boot, chill out, befriend local bandits, work on his Tumblr pics blog, maybe cyber-date a nice local girl back home.

But here he is in Bolivia, Illinois, in the midst of yet *another* romp with a Museum Program Director nearly three times his formal education level. He feels rudderless in the cauldron of this repeating compulsion. He sometimes thinks if he hadn't been introduced to the unpredictable pleasures of cross-class cultural education on his first two trips abroad (Canada, Ohio; Mexico, Indiana), that maybe he would have remained as he once was: scattered, adrift, venal. Instead, he now feels more decisive, focused, more driven than ever—a total slave—to *himself.*

This is his very first public, in the nude, high-rise window washer during a blizzard pic. He has no idea that this *non-erotic* image resides on thousands of hard drives worldwide. The Museum Program Director he "seduced" at the wine bar had carefully placed a camera lens into one of her private *Cristo Negro* statues on the dashboard of her Benz.

Two minutes after this pic was snapped, he uttered in his mind the phrase that always brings him to a decisive crossroads: "Noble Petronius, Arbiter of Taste to Nero, you of whom Nero demanded a doable suicide plan for you *from* you, I beseech you, gently intimate to me . . . is this . . . a *fucking real poetics*, or not?"

EL LECTOR

This being your one "casual" perusal too many, the one that tipped this *mildly* perverse book over the mountain ledge into a violent tumble, splintering pines, scattering birds, the pungent odor of pitch all around.

LAS COLEGAS

The idea of sharing her One God's Oneness hadn't even remotely appealed to her, but once this cavernologist colleague from Flagstaff, Arizona, turned her onto the Poly Gods' habit, she's all but lost the desire to go solo.

They've almost lost count of how many Poly Gods they've prayed to together. Besides the both receiving her One God's Oneness regular deposits of *absolute absence* into one or the other's souls, the cavernologists have been praying hard to at least two other Poly Gods' *zero absolute absence* per week—all unbeknownst to her One God's Oneness (which is likely, not possible).

One Poly God they pray hard to happens to be her colleague's former One God's Oneness (who also believes he's the One God's Oneness *as* the One); the other Poly God is the two One God Onenesses' *absolute absence* (for lack of a better word) "coach," who they've code named "Immanent Presence X."

Some evolutionary psychology research has speculated that totemic tale construction might have a mildly addictive quality, given that it helps regulate serotonin secretion rates, especially during ecstatic prayer. The cavernologists are not quite sure about that. What they are sure of, however, is that by (in their language) "schmooxing" copious amounts of *absolute absence* with dashes of faith, the energy effect of it is multiplied. The only problem they've detected is that the potency, from whichever Poly God's *absolute absence* they've schmooxed the longest, diminishes at twice the rate of any new Poly God's *absolute absence.*

This weekend, they're attending a mass prayer rally in Philadelphia. They've bought plane tickets, accommodations, etc. They're determined to recruit as many (in their language) "schmooxaneers" as they can manage, before returning to Flagstaff.

LOS ESPIAS

From: Pixter1000@hotmail.com
To: Suckerforsecrets@hotmail.com
Re: re: you owe me one

Dude, I hope this covers my "outstanding balance." We found it on Pyongyang's Chief Diplomat's cell log. It was from "Guzzler Guy 13"—a text, with an attachment. Fuck. If this wasn't enough of a mind-bender for me to be peering straight into my North Korean "strictly for public consumption" foreign policy glossary spread-sheet, to find out that the pic was snapped by my very own Chief of Communications—that—has me reeling. What the fuck! Are they in cahoots? I knew they both attended the same Home Brewing Seminar in Portland last summer, but I had no clue. Well, back then I didn't, but since then, a postcard from Taplands Jamboree 2011 came to the Oval Office, "Thanks for the Bellyful Barrels of Fun!"

Honestly, I wish I hadn't seen this, but I have to admit, that pic of your *Ministre de la Défense* handing the Ukrainian Minister of Trade Norway's "Getting around OPEC" petro-policy outline in The Strip Steakhouse men's b-room in lower Manhattan—gets me really going.

Dude, we're sickos to the max you and me, and it's good we'll never come to any public accord over Global Internet Security, so I'll add this to the hopper. Last night I took it *really* deep. I made go viral this vid of my Chief Diplomat to Barbados receiving from Barbados' Minister of Justice an envelope of Columbian Cartel protection money—and had the guy arrested on the spot—live! And now I'm looking to somehow get a staffer to post a pic of my U.N. representative's folio of Virgin Islands incentive benefits to Libya's outgoing *Al Wadan* of Mass-Public Moral Entertainment. Surely I'll go to hell for this.

LOS IDOLOS

The trapped vaporized ammonium atmosphere of this 6th moon of Saturn, Titan, has been causing this banished Earth god's last remaining reserves of Rapture Oils to ooze out of it for over 3,000 Earth years now. It's always loved pinching clods of minerals into figurines that walk & talk, but now the iridium residue left lingering on its fatigued fingertips is making it sicker and sicker. Also, by the time Saturn's light glows over the horizon (every 15 Earth days), it's pinched so many iridium figurines into being throughout the night that their combined clamorous walking & talking are sufficient to keep the god's nerves on edge for hours at a time. The banished god's nightly, oily submergence into a frozen methane lake produces a thin cloud of toxic fog that eventually kills off all but the hardiest of iridium figurines by Saturn up.

Two nights ago (30 Earth days ago), two of the surviving figurines (one might compare them to poolside towel guys at a Hilton Hotel on Earth, the chill factor, the schtick) had a pretty uncontrolled Hydrogen-3 fire going about a half Saturn mile south of the Iridium Production Area. The god fell in with them rather easily, plied by their tongue-and-cheek worship of it and vague, un-targeted chortling. The god gave in rather easily, more than it ever had before.

Soon, it was accepting two completely contradicting tales of its own origins, first from one figurine, then from the other, back and forth. It also kept both of them on the brink by spinning them tales about *it* being kept on the brink by *them* being kept on the brink by *it*—for what seemed like ages.

Suddenly, one of them sprung open a Titan Rapture Date (TRD), like the quick release of a stopped-up hose of liquid nitrogen straight into the god's (of what might be called on Earth) "mouth." The god immediately spit out the proposed prophecy, quickly turning to the other figurine, but only *half*-receiving that figurine's alternate TRD. Afterward, each figurine gave the banished god yet a third option: a one-way ticket to Jupiter's 15th moon, Adrastea. The god bade them a hasty goodnight, happy to submerge deep into its icy methane lake for the night.

Banishment in the company of these two surviving figurines is definitely getting interesting. Last night the three returned to the uncontrolled Hydrogen-3 fire area only to find a third survivor figurine getting harangued by two additional figurines (in Earth-speak, Econo-Lodge Motel front desk types) by *their* exact TRD's. The two original survivor figurines patiently waited their turn to unveil their latest TRD's. The god slowly slinked back to the Iridium Production Area, extremely disturbed by the sight of—well, Iridium figurines acting so weird in general, but also, by their *physical ugliness*, especially as lit up by the light of Saturn's 8th moon, Iapetus.

All figurines have since come to terms with each of their own rapturous garrulity. They've also collectively apprehended the banished god's newly demoted condition. Tonight, again, the whole bunch is going down to the uncontrolled Hydrogen-3 fire area together. In their way of thinking, (which is, of course, unrepresentable in *any* Earthly, hospitality industry language), the figurines—although they haven't expressly said so to each other, have not ruled out a figurine-to-figurine refiguring of The Rapture of Titan which would entail the prefiguring of *no gods*.

The current reigning Earth god will be attempting a rescue & return operation of the banished god tomorrow morning. One of the figurines has already predicted this occurrence and precise date, and, even if it's done so only by chance, it's sure to scare the *bejeesus* out of anyone who notices.

LA MEDITADORA

The heart rate spiking, the extremities of her fingers and toes electrified, the eyes popping wide open . . . nothing makes her feel more alive than having the phrase "Core American Values" toss her around, having "its way" with her, the whole of her being as a plaything for its mad desire.

The blue star-studded envelope containing the phrase appeared in her mailbox at work. She slipped it into her red-wavy-lines-on-white purse for later viewing in the Boeing 737 restroom.

Now, with jittery hands, she slowly opens it. Her breathing halts for a moment. It's the first time she's felt herself in that compressed, eternal-seeming moment.

Suddenly, as if commanded by a ghost, she goes down on all fours in the cramped stall and raises her lowermost spine up high while arcing her uppermost spine backwards as far it can go. In that position, she tunes out everything in her mind except for "Core American Values" and her hard breathing muffled by the Boeing 737's twin jet engines at cruising speed.

Ten minutes go by, and as the feeling of fainting increases to a fevered pitch, she slams her face into the stall door ten times to bring herself around.

With lingering pain in her supmorbital foramen and zygomatic skull bones, she relaxes for the rest of the flight until landing in Lansing, MI, where she'll resume her life as a porous and permeable life form who works in a synchronized manner alongside identically porous and permeable life forms across the globe.

EL DOMESTICADO

In hindsight, many in his large extended family might have guessed he would grow up to be a CEO of a night vision equipment developing company in Las Cruces, New Mexico. A true believer in whatever his heart tells him to do, whether it be National Defense Budget Expansion Justification, colored sand paintings of The Redeemer, or local native plant preservation, a deep fervor (bolstered by the nourishment of a close family) flows out of him like agave nectar.

His contralto pitched, sempre moderato tempo voice is magically persuasive; almost everything he utters elicits a desire in others to do allegro con fuoco, soprano range deeds. He once convinced a group of classmates in his elementary school in rural Vermont to be on the lookout for Canadian pennies in order to collect them, roll them up, and give them out at nearby assisted care facilities.

So why is he on a pair of 15 ft. aluminum stilts clunking down South Main Street waving a corporate tax loophole conductor's baton with his right hand at midday?

His redeemer resides in *all* beings, seen and unseen, standing and barely standing, and for now, this newfound dedication to privatizing Medicare entitlements (not being one who'd *personally* break into old folks homes—snatch their possessions and gamble them away at roadside casinos in Bernalillo and Sandoval counties) is out of sight of his redeemer's all-pervading radiant goodness.

He's also mindful of sending his wife out on little errands during his kids' naptime. A prestissimo con bravura cam-session with a very partial, non-redemptory friend from Fort Jackson, SC, Major-General Valerixa McMartinez II, makes for a perfect finale to the long week.

LA ESCULTURA

Timely, "terrible," *exquisite* deliverance in Concord, New Hampshire at The Great American Celebrity Making Retreat. Summerlong seminar gone bonkers: "I'm a phony," she says to herself every night before going to sleep. Deep down, she knows she's not. She is, in fact, a highly talented celebrity-maker in the making.

—I'm a phony.
—Yes, you are . . . and you need to *sculpt* that, right?
—Yes.
—You're like a pathogen crawling aimlessly on the surface of this planet. Only by breaking past cell membrane barriers do you grow.
—Yes.
—Stick your hand in that plaster.
—Yes.
—Lower.
—Yes.
—Yes what?
—Yes, please—make me a sculptor of celebrities.
—Put plaster on this platter for casting.
—Yes . . . *oh my god* . . . it's cold, grainy, messy.
—Sculpt!

—Yes . . . um . . . hm . . . ah *hah*.

—Now, *ask* for it.

—Yes . . . *please*, I need baking, I need to be baked.

EL DROGADICTO

"Dear Doctor A,

Ever since my eldest colony's traumatic first constitution-framing trip, he's been obsessed with having illuminated duplications made of himself worldwide. By my latest count, this must be his 235th duplication, a hologram, actually.

The nightmare began as he perceived himself to be eaten by flesh-eating (as he worded it) 'others,' little by little. This went on for two whole centuries. Next, his cities turned into 'mushroom-like protuberances;' then his borders were split open by 'thin lines from my puritan hips to my homeland rickety knees that opened into canyons of red flesh;' his legislative nipples then began spitting out a 'purple-colored goop' that dropped onto his executive belly; after that, 'a painful spiked tail' started coming out of his judicial tush-hole, lashing his congressional buns till they were 'bled white;' next, his foreign affairs neck started 'growing and growing' until it suddenly snapped forward plunging his head into its (oh my god, I can't believe I'm actually typing this, but it's *his* words) 'mother country's sweet slushy cone values fun hole' (mine!); at long last, before he passed out, after screaming bloody murder, 'the spiked tail whirled and whipped into my throat so deep that it reached the inside of my folkloric country stomach and started to eat it.'

He's all right now, I assure you. He has a nice job in a new international law office that he enjoys very much. Everything is fine except for these holographic illuminations he spends a good portion of his Gross Domestic Product on.

Do you think he needs therapy? Or medication? Or maybe—and this is what I'm thinking—a *much* older nation who makes him feel like a handsome aging buck *all* the time?

Sincerely Yours,

Mrs. Q."

LA GALERISTA

"I want to be well-known and influential for my conook-anák-anók-ka-ník-ník art, 'new-body' sculptural, photographic, and video work.

I was born in *Ooooooo*-la-mala-mula-manuna but moved to the United States at a young age. I've recently earned a kenooki-cooki-pooki-fanooki award from Stanford University, and my work will soon be presented in *Chiuuuu-shrrrr*-hiphiphip(hip).

Some consider my work to be strongly chawola-yamola, while others call me a sell-out of chawola-yamola. My early conook-anák-anók-ka-ník-ník art was focused on violence against the tooo-*ooon*-jajajajaja body. Lately, I've focused on a spiritual and physical connection with young tooo-*ooon*-jijijijiji bodies.

During the last two years, I've started creating 'body objects,' mostly sustained, live 'sculptures' of my body in bound positions. My aim is to maximize a ¡tandoo-ka-karán! of social-interactive intentionality in public spaces.

My upcoming performance involves ten tooo-*ooon*-jijijijiji who've all recently turned nineteen to deliver their yámbara-corúmbara-salah

50

into my *yooofff*—o' (o'). There is to be a minimally perceived break between one's yámbara-corúmbara-salah and another's. As soon as the lunga-saráf of one comes out, another one's lunga-saráf goes in. I remain silent throughout. As soon as the last one has yámbara-corúmbara-salah'd into me, they all get dressed and clear the space. I remain still for about ten minutes, holding in the small lake of yámbara-corúmbara-salah inside me. Then, in a gesture of newfound tooo-*ooon*-jajajajaja empowerment, I let gush out all of the pleasure that I harbored to myself (*for* myself) for all spectators to either critically evaluate, be disturbed by, or simply enjoy."

LA CREADORA

Moment one one-trillionth of one second, the quantum fluctuations of the infinitely dense glorious-mess-in-place awaiting cosmic expansion.

Out of the blue, she contacts her previous creation's collaborator, the maker of another universe eight dimensions infolded inside the dimension she's held sway over for more than 13.75 billion years. Their principal indulgence used to be her "exchanging" gravitons across energy membranes, confounding his energy-gravity "unified" super-field *thinkers*. For a half one one-millionth of one second before opening up the basic atomic conditions for life-business, *that* was "the deal." So this time, after chaos-calibrating her local universe's *bang* expansion-rate for one one-twentieth of one millionth of one second, she accepts all possible quark configurations to be uniformly distributed onto her universe's element-building potential, a near-zero energy constant conducive to hadrons lingering in—*bang radiance.*

They tidy themselves up, and she stays for about two one one-millionths of one second afterward, fine-tuning her dark-matter-to-sensate-matter ratio alongside other dimensions (namely, 1, 5, and 6). The two maintain a polite and formal demeanor while withholding their respective material knowledge natures from too hasty "forecasters" in their respective cosmic environs.

Moment 10^-43, non-leisurely, super-expansion, followed by "cool-down."

After five billion years of trawling for possible life forms in the supra dimensional "realities," she falls asleep ("asleep?" yes!). This being *the* indispensible atomic bonding moment with which all discernable organic matter can take form. Midway through this cosmic doze, she wakes up unable to go back to sleep. She punches out an enormous black hole next to two quasars and teases out a small dark energy vacuum filled with fresh nothingness. She takes a couple of deep hits. Once she feels it (the fresh nothingness) coming on, she transports her oldest, original light to the edge of the expansion horizon, and from the inner core of a lone, red giant collapsing star, gathers all of its deuterium. She transports it (or, rather quantum entangles it) to a spacious quadrant of her universe that's rich in anti-matter, and for five one one-millionths of one second, indulges in bright matter recombinatory *excess*, for the moment closing the door on all further "configurations," further "potentialities."

At the edge of her universe's theoretical expansion horizon-plane, she then violently transitions the deuterium into tritium before forming a helium nucleus ready to chain-react into hydrogen isotopes that will burn for—*a good long while.* After 1.5 billion years, a yellow-white star takes form. She patiently (imaginarily) keeps watch on the 28th satellite closest to that star with an (imaginary) ardent affection and (imaginary) heavy heart. On occasion, she stops by and lightly runs her (imaginary) hand across the bark of the oldest tree high above a canyon where a little stream trickles its way to a massive, restless ocean.

EL TRIO

This undocumented caretaker of young children was even younger than this when she first fell in with them. It was the NannyTemp Corp's Executive's assistant who first fancied her. The razor-sharp, early graying, "ultimate team guy," has a thing for "wild runaway" words with "perfectly controlled-chaotic" arguments. The executive felt very nervous and apprehensive at first, but when she saw that "tsunami mouth" (as they call her) had an unquenchable need to be "of use" in every imaginable way, she relaxed into her role.

It usually starts by the assistant looking down at his own rather sizable feet, and reaching down towards his clogs to remove them, each clog tucking in a brown, acrylic, highly flammable "footie." As the first clog comes off, the assistant reaches into the long-abandoned mines of his activist, "idealist 90's" memory banks. The very sight of the nanny's sledgehammer-grade palms and pavement-pounded sweat from a 10-hour workday drives the assistant into a tailspin of ethnic/sexual contra *dictions*. By now, the nanny's nearly detectable scowl coupled with her "corporate advertisement poetic skills" has rendered the pair both silly numb (or, numbly silly).

The executive then introduces her own taquitos-to-*tacotes* success story deep into the nanny's—well, *actual* poetry reading at The Met—*as*—the assistant glides his swift bare feet over a mauve mahogany dance floor co-articulating her sledgehammer-grade words with every step.

The nanny then lets loose a torrent of *New Experimental Latina Literature* as the assistant's detached tongue glides across the cactus frond of his worst self-doubts. Next, the harsh sound of the exec's purse zipper opening, releasing "executive wisdom" makes the nanny's inspired belly quiver even more. They then gently collapse her poetic persona limb by limb until she lay prostrate on the ground. As if on cue, she opens her larynx extra wide. Slowly, the director's story starts to come out, but in contorted, barely comprehensible tongues.

They keep her going like this for a long time; they take their time with her, paying close attention to media-viral potential. Her eyes roll back into her head as she feels her first wave of temporary revolutionary ecstasy. The exec and her sidekick are both very practiced at knowing exactly when she's most likely to—*join a union*. And just as her entire body starts to flood with a sense of *bloody purpose*, the exec "professionally delivers" hot tips of "savvy sense" onto the surface of the nanny's "outdated aesthetic concept." The assistant then sops up the temporary overflow, especially focusing on the unpredictable contours of "tsunami mouth's" words.

EL MUSICO

Auditioning to be in the sternum bones section with the Boston symphony is in itself an accomplishment, and although it's been very nervous about it, it's been tingly with pride all week.

The guest dormitory is very small, but as sleek as any room it's ever stayed in. The mattress is thick and very inviting.

Although it's gained 200 pounds in the last three months, this Gorilla (this Gorilla in this dormitory room) noticed that it appeals to a completely different set of people than it's normally used to, very sophisticated people, actually. So, for the moment, it feels adequately appreciated.

Tonight, it's going for a *double-fist 100 all-scales pump compounder*, perhaps the biggest one to date. It feels like it really needs this rehearsal. The big ones—if it's ready for them—work wonders for it. They give it confidence, a sense of self-control, but also a sense of ultimate surrender.

It'll employ one mattress on each wall, plus one above to drown out the scales.

The repertoire it's playing tomorrow is well known to all classical musicians, amateurs and professionals alike. Its aim is to play with great deliberateness, balancing restraint with flights of rhythmic fancy.

LOS COMBATENTES

In 3055 A.D., the Eximmigramanid Empire of The Three California's great commander, Guigo, led an ill-fated campaign against the New American League in which he was roundly defeated at the Battle of Las Vegas. After the terrible fighting subsided, two isolated units from either side found themselves in an over-impacted suburb on the borders of what's now the modern nation of Canexico. They eventually settled into a common Planetary Neutral Zone (PNZ), incorporating the surrounding New American League's battleweary people into a new league. Eventually, their league too was absorbed by the larger Greater Pacific Production Zone (GPPZ), and so on, and so forth.

Countless males and females since then have kept the semen and ovules "flowing" and "colliding" in underground nitrogen chambers powered by harnessed sub-mantle magma drifts rechanneled for power distribution. By night, the isolated genes of 21st century politicians and drug-addicted beauticians alike have kept excited young lab experimenters "amped up" as altered DNA sequences rescramble during "lightening storms" of "hard," "explorative" synthetic gene infusions; everyone shudders with every "woosh-woosh" cycle. By day, those same reconstituted pools (XX's *as*

YY's) are cryogenically preserved in vials, then sealed and stored into satellites that rotate around AM22 (artificial moon 22), until a given PS (planetary sector) is due for "repop."

An only child's comfortable sleeping quarters in a capsule hexagonon high above Old York City's Borough of New Prince, is a long way from that long-forgotten, over-impacted suburb on the borders of Canexico, but the *energy* from that over-impacted suburb speaks of an indisputable victory.

LOS COCHES

Different enamel shine coatings, different tints and textures of upholstery, one's trunk slightly fuller than the other's, same rapid fuel injection systems, same exhaust intake manifolds . . .

Washington DC, Spring, 2011 . . . cars are becoming *perfect pals* these days, cooperating in netting as many families to ride in them as they can manage.

After decades of rotating long shifts, hosting cheery men and women at their primary residence, the Senate Chamber, each getting lightly groped by different National Energy Plans, they share a little moment of relaxation.

Next week they'll be on overtime . . .

A yearly hydrogen & hybrid electric strip revue in Detroit is on the calendar.

LOS FAMILIARES

"Dear 'Lil' Discourse,'

Ever since your phrase, 'mediating my identities,' has been stay-
ing with us in Western Texas, it's uh . . . well, I'm kind of embar-
rassed to report this . . . but it's um, become . . . more than a bit of
a . . . *tramp* (ouch)"

—As ever yours, your affectionate, older universalist-humanist
discourse

"Thanks for relating this, sis, seriously. I'm so glad we're in contact
again, and this time, with some kind of *higher* purpose! ('a long
break from its usual campus scene' as you originally put it).

But, what exactly do you mean, 'tramp?' Ok, the reel of it shooting
everyone in the mall obviously bespeaks of a 'risqué,' hyper self-
identified *logic,* but . . . it's just what young free logics do these
days, no?"

—As ever yours, "Lil' Discourse"

"Dear 'Lil' postmodern, fractalled-relativist, non-unitary discourse'
—listen,

You surely must know I'm still quite surprised *and* delighted (still! after 21 years) that you decided to raise a radically modular phrase like, 'mediating my identities' in the first place, right? But your naiveté astounds me. I feel I have to tell it to you like it is. It . . . is a fast-talking, fast-moving, web 2.0, little *fuck machine* —on the loose.

The app-adding, stat-compounding, cyberwolf howling to the swollen, silver prairie moon *antics*, keep us awake late into the night—nightly."

"Jeepers, sis, I actually suspected as much. Is there anything in this entire world that I can actually do?"

"Honestly, no."

LA IMAGEN

Neither she nor anyone else has yet thought of a truly compelling storyline to go with this image of herself scrunched into a corner of a boutique in the Chelsea District after closing hours wearing a royal blue Hazmat suit and black gas mask reading a 1971 yellow OSHA standards catalogue—backwards.

Who is she? Is she merely someone's (doctored, distorted) "weirdly gorgeous" poetic offspring, or is she something more than that?

Alright, if she is "something much more than that," then why is regarding her as "someone's (doctored, distorted) 'weirdly gorgeous' poetic offspring" the thing that *really* kicks your "media intelligence" into high gear?

Whether you're a "global leader in the embroidery industry" or a "local enforcer of dangerous workplace practices," or just a pooped-out liberal littérateur in New York City who *imagines* both of those, when viewing this image (royal blue—black—yellow) the idea of re-pixellating images one upon the other for twelve hours a day in a sparsely decorated cubicle alongside three hundred others in Mumbai, is something that might not get your attention.

To actually *feel* yourself turned into re-pixellated portions of an anonymous force's self-image, switch-packeting you onto the internet just as you're about to declare a lyrically lush "love of humanity in general"—is something that *could* grab your attention, but also make for a pretty damn good "(doctored, distorted) 'weirdly gorgeous,' poetic offspring" in need of a storyline.

EL GRUPITO

Meal for history

Estimated time of underground syndicate's existence: 1 year, 3 months

Number of full-blown, media-diffracting actions: 38

Human faculties sharpened/perfected: oculatory, olfactory, gustatory, somatosensory

Amount of doublethink: zero

LOS BARDOS

The edge of death

The seconds right before the cessation of *all* sensation. Biologic systems breaking down, a *narrowing* of the Life Force, heading towards some kind of conclusion, a "conclusion" whose conditions remain *utterly unknown* to the living.

Death—is not "a black void in eternity."

To begin with, the word "black" requires a monosyllabic utterance; it is formed by the lips, tongue, and throat of the living.

First, a soft-labial explosive is formed by the lips; it is then followed by a soft flicking of the tongue at the roof of the mouth; that, in turn, is followed by an opening of the glottis (the tongue is passive at that moment, the lips are passive at that moment); the word ends with a rapid compression of the tonsils into a final crisp, clicking sound, "k."

All that's not death—is a sure candidate for being "life"

"Two people read a sonically virtuosic dialogue, eagerly devouring & variating each other's rhythm's for the first time."

RADIANCE OF ONE ENTITY TRANSPORTING ANOTHER ENTITY INTO ANOTHER REALM

EL PSICOLOGO

Ditching a whole week of classes in the middle of his first semester at Oberlin to spend it in Belarus with his dorm building's maintenance man is a dicey proposition to be sure. Telling his new girlfriend he's going to his grandmother's funeral in "nowhere Pennsylvania" while at the same time asking his parents for $1,000 for a "social activism retreat in the state of Washington"—is even more dicey.

But those things pale in comparison to him accepting $10,000 to transport eight packets of T4 explosives in his intestines "to be deposited" in the privacy of a hotel room next to Newark International Airport.

It's his third time, and like the other two times, everything went as smooth as glass.

The following weekend after he got back, he took a bus to New York City to spend some "alone time." In the Meat Packing District (where the Hollywood set flies in to shop) he bought a black, sharkskin pair of pants with a sparkly silver trimmed belt for $2,000.

In the cellar of his dorm room, the oil-burning heater makes a deep whirring sound just loud enough to drown out the latest round of tactical arguments led by the maintenance man's storm of demonic words. After the kid's "collegiate-global opinion" has withstood a solid forty-minute pounding, he respectfully slips out of the cellar and changes into the black sharkskin jeans and sparkly silver trimmed belt for a "night out on campus" (poorly lit).

Next morning, in the cafeteria, he greets his girlfriend with an easy smile. They stroll out onto a large grass lawn in the warm sun to study for their psychology final, "multiple personalities diagnosis." He announces to her that he's decided to specialize in that very area. She slowly clasps his hand and gives him a little peck on the lips.

LOS RESIGNADOS

"Oh my god, I was—for a flash of a moment—so jealous when I looked across the room and saw you getting *pre-published* by that weird guy with the black gloves, but I have to admit, ever since that evening, I can't get the image of your hummingbird-like flightiness and form-fibrillating *social graces* out of my mind.

We've been 'scenester & scenestress' for 42.731 years now, but I think it's time we give in to this new reality. I know you crave new hokey poetic trends—donkey-eared ones, short rhino-tailed ones, toucan-hooking crooked ones, one's with huge swollen gizzards a-flapping for all to see.

When that up-and-comer 'oral tradition' specialist from the South Bronx introduced his *Poesia Auténtica Revolucionaria de Nuestras Americas* perspective into your well-worn repertoire and yanked off your remaining 'urban hair piece' while you screamed 'de-wig me!' Then him scattering your ceramic craftworks onto the floor, pruning your prize-winning tulips at will—*clip clip clip clip*—then class-roasting your boating friends as we were about all aboard—eyebrows nearly seared off—eyes glazed as the sun set—and you, squeezing your wine glass stem till it snapped—at that point, right there, I knew you weren't the same 'scenetress' I ran with 42.731 years ago.

I can't wait to hear your true feelings about all this under the cover of a dense, thick layer of CO_2 cloud cover in Poughkeepsie, NY.

With Love,

Yr. Corporate, lightly-literary, handy husband"

LAS CONVENIENCIAS

"There . . . mmm . . . that should settle me down for a few weeks . . . ouch . . . *mmm* . . . oof! I really needed that . . . I really *need* this kind of stuff! . . . so much . . . I'm glad tech commodities just *blend into reality itself* when their initial wow-moment is finished—bastards! . . . they so . . . get me going . . . what they *do* to me . . . I don't think I'm able to . . . pay much attention to anything . . . just now . . . even if I tried (ha!) . . . god, it *works!* this app . . . I fucking *love it* . . . I love it I love it I love it . . .

Tomorrow I'll:

√ Rotate my egalitarian value-system to align with connect-me-first residues smeared onto my heart's dresser mirror

√ Clean out the old political refrigerator

√ Re-write my resume

√ Update my profile on meetahotnewephemeralproduct.com

√ Write a poem—I haven't *penned* one in over a year!

√ Apply some high quality skin lotion to my sizzling, sweet, touch-pad index finger flesh"

LOS ENTUSIASTAS

This has gone pretty far, and it's likely to go farther. Quite literally nothing else does it for them anymore—they have to feel fully airborne and free falling to the ground—to feel anything at all.

How did this deep-seated understanding of body mass vs. gravity evolve?

When they're Corporate Assets Chief finally let them control the main console a few nights at the Federal Aviation Center's Jet Lander Simulator last year, these *barristers* were absolutely smitten with aerospace near-miss disasters. They suddenly felt internally chaotically frisky, suddenly more the captains of their primal instincts.

They wore mostly twill and tight button-down long sleeves as they depressed & released literally hundreds of buttons per session. One night, unbeknownst to them as to why, they decided to wear fireman pants, but sheared-off, in the form of a kilt, cut just above the knees. As they pre-sequenced what seemed like just another routine flight from La Guardia to Ronald Reagan International, they suddenly sensed an intense heavy gaze fall onto their faces from across the hangar. No sooner than they looked up to see who it was, than they sensed a huge stream of piss dropping onto their "pants." They immediately (electro-mechanically) deployed a towel from under the consoles and began to frantically wipe themselves off. As the wiping came to a close, they raised their heads only to find the man with the deep-set eyes and oddly angular Hollywood plastic-looking dark hair carving out their skulls with his gaze. They felt additional drops sprinkle onto their *mixed up* attire. The rest is history.

They've grown to love the combination of charred, "preferred guest" lawyerly aroma coupled with the light, sprizzy scent of liquid nitrogen foam and polyethylene anti-incendiary tarps. They all play hard at "trap the union health & safety department into a genie bottle."

Also, they've since switched from twill & graph paper pattern wear to modest platinum leopard pants and chunky-monkey muscle tees at headquarters. They're not "casualties," they're casualty *makers* and *shakers.*

LA RATONSITA

The future, for the moment, looks very bright. Ten minutes from now, she'll momentarily be putting aside twenty years of a mindful, carefully planned, "high functioning" values-instilling upbringing, exchanging it for a half paragraph of poetic prose written on a damp beer coaster at noon.

Chug n' scribble, seven days a week, twice a day, that's the deal. Once in the morning, starting at 9:00 a.m. (at the emeritus professor's faux dive bar, before he speeds off to the Danbury Heliport in Connecticut en route to Barnard College in upper Manhattan), and once in the evening, starting at 6:00 p.m. (at this same professor's boutique beer tasting establishment two doors down, as he heads home to his "protective hearth").

Tab's on the house.

There's three coffeehouses in town where she spends the rest of her day meditating on novel-writing strategies. Hopping from one coffeehouse to the other, she doesn't give her morning and evening "jobs" a second thought. She's a great tipper. The kids love her.

On weekends, she often runs into her former prof and his little family on Main Street. "Coffeehouse rats" is what his wife calls them, secretly envious of all the time they have to read and write.

Once in a while the wife sees this particular "rat" decked out in fake pearls and fake fine linens having a bottle of wine by herself at the Tuscan Taverna.

Last week, she worked up the nerve to ask the young lady what kind of novel she was writing.

"The title of it is, 'Wife Trap.'"

"Oh . . . do you have a *contract* for it?" she asked, in a biting tone.

"I do. Thanks for asking."

LAS ATLETAS

"Take *that,* miss True-Feminine USA, 'potential amusement park industry business partner after grad school.'

Actually, you're worth the whole five rounds *right now*—just as you are—idealistic, malleable, shuffling, plus your right hook is definitely worth a run.

Bring it—com'on! *Boom!*

That's it . . . *boom—bam—boom* (nice)

Certainly you'll hark back to these underground Muay Thai gambling dens in El Paso when your McMansion lifestyle is closing in on you in the suburbs of Birmingham, someone always complimenting on your 'enviable homemaking skills.'

Sweet brute—*bring it*!

(Your mom, by the way, was the best embroidery (slash) AR15 semi-automatic target practice instructor I ever had. Bless her heart.)"

LA FUTURISTA

Lipids are known to spontaneously form bilayered vesicles in water. Perhaps a deep sea-vent's compression of amino acid-rich heated lime with hyper-oxygenated carbon could have produced the needed single fatty acid chain per lipid that constituted the first cell, the first real form of "information" on the planet, a catalytic synthesis of new proteins that in a billion years time evolved into the millions of specialized cell groups needed to constitute complex specialized bodies.

The green day-glo tag on her wrist is from Coco's Tropicana Dance Hall at the Holiday Inn, in Des Moines, Iowa. This convention has been just *amazing*. She's never had as much fun as this, never met as many interesting people. Her legs are heavy as tree trunks from all the dancing. Her head is both fuzzy and ultra sharp, a potent result of the blazing lectures and rum-fueled nights. The entire area between her temporal to parietal lobes all the way down to her cerebellum is completely neuron-fire-ready, relaxed and open to whatever day or night might bring.

Vulcanism's residue, this genetic engineering principal investigator from North Dakota.

EL QUIMICO

The generalized sense of terror he feels for household cleaning products—ever since he can remember—melts away at times like this. This is why he goes for this kind of stuff.

As to what the seven 300 gallon tankards of different bathtub cleansers crowding in around him are feeling as they spray, spew and spill onto him—over and over—whatever *that* may be, he doesn't think about nor does he care about it in any way.

A nonpublic online album serves as an archive for these rituals. The link is known only to and used by sixteen other *domicilio-cleanso-phobes*, sixteen senior chemical engineers who are similarly wired. They've never met in person, but they communicate on an almost daily basis. They refer to it as SSR, or "sacred suds ring."

The site currently houses 50 posts. One of the "followers," who also happens to be a natural gas liquids specialist, has estimated the approximate total amount of cleansers shed by the "protector angel" tankards to be around three and one half metric tons.

LA PROLETARIA

The smell of pulp, turpentine and bleach usually permeates this side of town. But when winds from the southeast swoop into the valley, the toxic brew is fast cleared away, and what remains is the smell of wet grasses, mud, and wild flowers. This natural phenomenon mitigating human-made conditions has only a limited effect on the minds of the hard-working townsfolk whose every other thought dotes on the health and growth of the town's young.

She not only had the gall to admit it to herself, but also had the presence of mind to look for an opening (any) to construct a whole new reality for herself, and for *something else*. The eerie attraction she felt for this outcropping of Pre-Cambrian rock spoke clearly and directly to her the first time she saw it in the middle of the field.

In the deep of winter, the paper mill's indoor facility is cold and noisy. In that environment, she didn't pay much attention to the roll press feeder guy dressed in the mustard-colored industrial pants and brown checkered long sleeve felt shirt. Also, the safety glasses and helmet occluded much.

One day, her workmate buddy approached her about the possibility of maybe coaching her "little cousin" on basic lacrosse techniques. She readily agreed, having been a great player in school herself, the same school her buddy's "little cousin" was now attending, but also the Pre-Cambrian rock in the middle of the field, enabling her resolve.

Actually, she recognized him before he did her. She had caught his eye at the mill. She thought he was "cuddly," but sufficiently "rough," her exact taste in "little cousins," which was just beginning to pick up speed. Decked out in a bright red, terry cloth, short sleeve disco shirt, and loose-fitting green parachute pants, the only part of him she could correlate to the Pre-Cambrian rock in the middle of the field *and/or* the guy at the press feeder on the third shift—the general mass and approximate density, was *something else*. She could barely cloak the dilation of her cheeks' surface arteries as she laughed easily at herself flaying the lacrosse stick every which way, tumbling to the ground, legs all over the place.

At the end of practice, she offered to give him a ride home. As fate would have it, hard rains had made the winding road where "little cousin" lived impassable. They had to turn onto "the estuary," the oldest road in this part of central Missouri, a tree-lined road made of stone and railway planks.

The sound of the automobile's front axle rod snapping in two reached her ears pretty much at the same time as *something else* crawled its way up into her nostrils. The last moment of sanity she remembers is the look of her own short brown hair flared out onto her face in the mirror, sticky and messy, the Pre-Cambrian rock in the middle of the field there also. As a whole new reality set in, a gust of wind made the maples around them rustle.

EL CHILE

After it stopped photosynthesizing carbon dioxide for twelve hours a day and quit its stringent water acquisition routine from its underground root system some twenty meters away, it's settled down enough to where it could give it some real thought.

It *loves* the feel of its newly vine-clipped torso, how it sleekly harbors two seed-snuggling membranes that face each other in damp darkness; even more than that, it basks in the smell of its burnt, mood-altering, capsaicin filling up a whole room. So that's that, it's completely committed to this slower, more sensual way of being.

The important thing now is to tune up its radar for humans who really appreciate a vegetable like this. The more genuine desire the human shows (no matter what standing in society that human has, as long as that human has good hygiene and manners) the more it happily allows itself to be consumed like a six course enchilada dinner with honey-dipped fry bread in a piñon-roofed, shaded patio in Santa Fe.

EL CABALLERO

"Honestly, I bungled the whole thing—from beginning to end. To begin with, the deceased president I summoned through the Great Central Wormhole and had re-particalized right here in your workspace—was the wrong fucking guy!

What's the probability of two deceased presidents with such similar avatars in one's wormhole intake platform—'makerofsouls' vs. 'maskerofsouls.' I got stuck with 'masker!' *Phew.* What a ride! What a piece of work this guy. See this shit I'm wearing? That was just the beginning of the night. And how do you like me in (as he called them) 'sugared piggy tails.'

I knew things were getting pretty weird when he made me crawl on my hands and knees from the Oval Office to the Blue Room gallery and made me 'meow-bark' like a 'dog-cat' at a portrait of James K. Polk, after McKinley arguably the most Bush-like 'adventurous' type before, well, you.

As if things couldn't get more surreal than that (I, of course, went along with all of it, like I promised you I would, Mrs. President), the wormhole re-particulated image of his half-decapitated neck holding up a fully decomposed face working its way into my tense, apprehensive eyes, almost had me running out onto the Great Lawn for air. He then had me 'cow-howl' (I did this too) as he 'wolf-woofed' at a bust of Gorbachev in the basement below the Red Room (ever been there?). Surprisingly, after twenty minutes or so, I calmed down and sort of . . . *got into* this 'off the record' National Teaching Moment.

Anyway, miss you *dearly,* and can't wait till you're back home from your 'Micronesian Islands in full support of Israel' tour.

XOXO,

Your most devoted, first gentleman."

LA RECREACIONISTA

The more unrecognizable she becomes to herself, the more it makes her feel alive. It's her biggest secret. She's never so much as even hinted it to anybody. Usually, people spill secrets in small amounts, a little bit of the truth here, a little bit over there. Not her. This thing is in lockdown.

She's been booking the same abandoned Creamscicle ® warehouse refrigerator once a month for over two years. She checks in at 3:00 pm, and goes at it until 2 or 3 in the morning. Her suitcase is filled with vintage 1950's male corporate clown icon outfits she's carefully ordered online. Everything fits perfectly as she puts them on. This achievement in itself is what awakes her fundamental apprehension of the Tea Party Movement, which builds and builds as the night progresses.

There are two mini-portable funhouse mirrors she places into this abandoned Creamsicle ® refrigerator, one on the ceiling, and one on the gray concrete floor below. The lighting resembles the white klieg lights of a 20's movie set. She starts off at room temperature and lowers the thermostat 10 degrees every hour.

This, here, is the very last vintage 1950's male corporate clown icon outfit she's donning for the night. After carefully adjusting the arm ruffles so that they're perfectly uneven, and meticulously arranging the waist ribbon girdle so that it makes her quadruple-sized *donk* seem detached from the rest of her body, she ties the size 18 shoes in such a way as to render her toes *ultra*-moveable—in any direction. Lastly, the slight tickle of the red bandana around her neck reminds her to keep very still, as nothing must move except for her grapefruit-orange & frost-blue eyelids.

The historical comprehension she feels for the Authentic American Entity she's gazing at begins to increase, breath by breath. Controlling her stomach so that it doesn't move, and "secretly" squeezing her pelvic muscles, while inspecting the thousands of cold dimples on the surface of her kneecaps, eventually brings her to a sudden, explosive, broad-implicative, *creation moment.*

EL FINANCIERO

This much needed break from visiting his new boss's extended family over the holidays has taught him some important things:

Small amounts of his own vocabulary (even though there's *no such thing*) on the tips of several strangers' tongues can be rather "attractive."

Being "pregnant" with "the reality" of "current conditions" means you can't get "pregnant" again (he knew this before, of course, but not like this).

Stepping into a high-end, after-trading hours aggro-male bar wearing a black bow tie and spaghetti-thin suspenders during a financial meltdown at two in the morning at the beginning of a new quarterly earning period gets you a *limited amount* of attention.

Booking an extended stay at a five-star hotel in Dubai in advance of a congressional inquiry using a moneygram from Aruba—is nearly impossible to trace.

EL AUTOR

The fact that he's dead doesn't horrify them anymore. On the contrary, it turns their loose pub chatter into stone-solid philosophic inquiry—so hard, they can plunge *any* topic straight into a dry, pyrite-dense creek bed, and have that topic—feel little pain.

They first caught sight of his paper-white, bloodless lips straddling the edge of a half-liter mug—bent over a bacteria-varnished oak counter in a rickety stool, just as the sun dipped below the horizon. As he stood upright, the carbonation in his mug made no motion whatsoever. With no expression on his face, he looked at them as if through them. He then glided towards them. Their hearts seemed to almost stop, and their hairs stood on end as he got closer.

Slowly, he unzipped his wafer thin, rectangular black canvas bag, revealing the aluminum silvery glow of a 15-inch Mac Book Pro, so bright it lit up all the half-liter mugs like candles around it. Frozen in fear, they became suddenly self-conscious of their shiny, black, squeaky, double-decker width Toshiba 18-inchers, how they were aching, reaching out towards . . . an Indianapolis 500 racing decals vibe. They were shocked to see the former "fire-wire" slit along the edge of his "Pro" replaced by the new "thunderbolt" mini-hole, a peripheral that can *barely* be seen from a "casual" side-angle view.

He had locked his sight straight into their eyes. They felt paralyzed. An intense heat began to radiate inside their chaotic, random chatter, a feeling of pressure that felt like a boulder of fool's gold lodged deep in their guts.

He then opened his mouth so wide that it seemed his lower jaw was going to separate from his face. They heard a soft, raspy, James Olmos-like voice—not in their ears, but in their minds, "feed me, *carnales.*"

The hot pressure inside each of them then turned into an ice-cold sensation. Then, like a keg valve snapped open, like a tap feeder-hose filling up with liters of natural springs water drowning in live yeast—flowing so smoothly and so fast out of a large, decorative porcelain tap handle, they thought their very kidneys would soon be "tapped" in like form.

The sight of his 15-inch Mac Book Pro drenched in a spew of hop-infused barely water, and him lifting the half-liter mug to his face, inhaling the excess foam from its edge, made a single tear of joy run from each one of their eyes.

He then slowly sank back into the rickety wooden stool at the bacteria-varnished oak counter, a film of Red Copper Imperial Ale staining his paper-white, bloodless lips.

LA BESTIA

Hauling men and women on its iron-grated, thrashing back from the Mexican/Guatemalan border to Zacatecas where its strange freight hop onto other brain-rattling, limb-churning, grain transport carts—making them grip its back with every twisting 1, 000 miles of motion—*not* feeling the veins on their necks expand—*not* being able to hear what they're praying for as the black exhaust blows into their faces—*not* sensing their ten-minute cat nap dreams conjuring up El Norte—*not* seeing fresh blood spilled on its tracks behind it—all these, make "the beast" (as migrants call this iron commodity transport serpent) even *harder.*

Its mechanical design engineers could never in a million years have guessed all these added functions, let alone a literary abstraction of it. Currently appointed Immigration Policy architects, on the other hand, have noted the ten city-blocks long contraption's penchant for producing black body bags in the expanse of Arizona deserts.

LAS NARCAS

"Here's the 'designer drug' warlock she's been cooking things up with behind my back. And like I told you, besides these (why Polaroid? right?) snapshots infuriating me, punching a deep hole into my stomach, they also make my NarcoWoman sense of self, tense with excitement. They intrigue me to my very bones.

I want to leach those pills for all their phenethylamines. I want to collect as much of the extracted epinephrine into my wholesale stock as I can. I want to cut it, bump it, and trick it into my own brand as quickly as I can.

Phew! Oh my god, it's such a relief to be confessing this to someone, but most of all to you. This thing we have of telling each other everything is—I agree with you—the only way we could have remained Civic/Governmental collaborators for as long as we have.

I think one of the main reasons I'm staying with this *particular* witch is to discover more of her secrets—secrets really do it for me, I don't know why.

Speaking of secrets, or rather, the revelation of secrets, a specific one, actually, I have to confess something to you, and I know it'll make you furious for a while, but I just have to tell you.

I've been rapid-separating N-methyl-1-phenylpropan-2-amine with this new 'warlock' of my own, and I'm really into it. It's been going on for about—well, for some time now. I would have told you earlier, but I had to test the local market first (plus decapitate about two dozen local 'bombitas' runners without any interference—like the last time).

Our first warlocky encounter happened the very night after you and I had that amazing early evening Just-Us-Narcas buffet in that cantina in Nuevo Laredo, the one with Xmas lights adorning the ceiling. I know this might sound awful to say, but tequila-talking it through with you really loosened me up to try completely new things with this fully globalized warlock.

Ok, so to be true to the deal that you and I have, that one or the other has to relate at least one specific detail of every new trade secret encounter, here it is:

We've been delivering 'coca'—without coke! We set up some of our own foot soldiers to media-showy arrests before ramping up operations at the crossing points. I've directed loads and loads of the cheap product deep into the U.S.—as far as Roanoke, Virginia. And I love it! I want *more* penetration! I love it when random, anonymous gringos croon 'Ehn ree-ah-lee-dad, yoh-noh soy oon adictoh.'

So that's where I've been on Monday, Wednesday, and Saturday nights of every month for the last eight months . . .

!A thousand narco-besos!

Your Civic/Governmental partner for life,

'Chata'

PAN (former PRI) candidate for senator from Tamaulipas."

LOS SOCIOLINGÜÍSTICOS

Studying rongorongo script at the University of Idaho can get very alienating. The script has, as yet, remained undeciphered. Nonetheless, engaging it *hardcore* can also radically loosen the fabric of one's handed down social values and actual practices. His Danish roommate has dealt very effectively with this predicament since she was about age ten, moving from country to country with her archeologist parents. She's learned how to momentarily shatter precisely this kind of alienation, fusing "lost" cultural threads into entirely new ways of being.

On "Easter Island" / Rapa Nui, they call it rongorongo, glyphs inscribed onto irregularly-shaped wooden tablets. The last writers & readers of it perished at the hands of those who were devoted to the Judeo-Roman Aramaic-to-Koine-Greek script commonly known in English as "The New Testament." After scoring a copy of it in an outdoor market in the capital city of Hanga Roa on the way home after a long day at the (now defunct) "Campo de Amigos de la Isla de Pascua," she stuffed it in her tote bag for later viewing. Thirteen years later these two script-deciphering students sitting on the edge of the Dane girl's futon, cracking open the English version of those ancient codices from The Levant alongside two dozen hi-resolution negatives of rongorongo, feel *fired up* by their phonemic-introgressive, cross-derivational methodologies.

Within an hour or so, the Judeo-Roman stuff had traveled straight to the center of their analytical reasoning faculties, only to spill out of their ears like Brits out of a pub at 11:00 p.m. "out for the night." The boy from just outside of Baltimore fell straight onto his back laughing hysterically when it became apparent there was a *total lack* of a single correlation between any carving on the tablets to a single verse line from the Levantine corpus—nor to *any* society that's come in between the two scripts in question. His chest still heaving, his core body temperature slightly elevated, the saliva on his tongue flooding his mouth then quickly drying up, he recomposed himself for a moment.

"Oh my god . . . yes, I'm ok. I can sit up, no worries . . . *oh my god . . . phew!* . . . how are *you* doing? Me too, I feel like . . . eating my own fingers, ripping my hair out . . . this is . . . *incredible* . . . what? Yeah—I feel like taking my pith helmet off too . . . shit . . . these safari shorts also have to come off . . . there . . . I'm *still* burning up . . .

Sure, tell me whatever . . . what? You're a 'trans-millenialistic' thinker? . . . I didn't . . . yeah, I'm cool with it, totally, really . . . me? No . . . I mean, I don't really know, I've never— you—*have*—right? Yeah? You like it? Really? That's cool . . . how many foundational civilization creeds have you—I dunno—*done*? Wow, you really like 'ranging,' huh? That's cool . . . uh, *sure*, I've thought about re-transcribing at a sub-script level . . . *um* . . . well . . . going down to the graphemic level, I guess . . . you've . . . yeah? So you enjoy that? Specifically I mean . . . *interesting* . . . interesting . . . 'playful seriousness' . . . yeah, I suppose I haven't really tried giving a name to my, uh, 'professional take' on it all—but yeah, that's what I dig about rongorongo, actually . . . a dive—into a wild, entangled unknown . . . More? Ok, just a few more verses from this . . . Judeo-Roman compendium of fuzzy-historical 'lost' cultural functions . . . ok ok, here goes . . .

Oh . . . *oh my god, yes* . . . I'm so still burning up . . . my gut feels almost herniated by all this . . . wuh? . . . um . . . no no— it's . . . totally cool . . . no, I mean, yeah, actually—um, I *do* wanna try it—I do . . . yes, I'm sure . . . in whatever, however—you think is—good . . . extrapolate away . . . please, *problematize* my methodogy . . . yeah I really want you to do that . . .

Whoa . . . this is working, huh? . . . you *do* have a . . . pretty wicked hypothesis on late eco-collapse signification systems there—for sure . . . keep rockin it! . . . uh . . . *hm* . . . I guess, yeah, I'd give it a few more logarithmic go-arounds . . . um . . . *sh' yeah*! fuckin' . . . *who wouldn't* love parallelistic derivational graphemic equivalencies . . . *yup* . . . oh my god, you might be onto something really big here, seriously."

LA MARATONISTA

Inflamed metatarsophalangeal joints had never occurred to her as something to even think about, something to mull over in great detail, let alone something to dote on with deep affection, something to *gift* to people whose devotional admiration of inflamed metatarsophalangeal joints borders on religious ecstasy.

She can spot them a mile away now. The way their pupils lock in and dilate at first sight of their terrifyingly demanding object of study. They're slaves, actually, slaves that willingly submit to their bonded condition; the more they prostrate themselves before the alter, the more *bountifully free* they feel!

This strange new world that she's since committed to fully exploring was first introduced to her by accident, by a total stranger, at an unexpected time. The odd thing is, is that she wasn't wearing carbon electron free-radical released, polyurethane blue & gold racing shoes, but fair-trade cotton vegan sandals when the stranger stopped her as she strode across the Broadway and 42nd street crosswalk, northwest corner.

YES, she *had* felt those emotions locked in her inflamed metatarsophalangeal joints for a long time. YES, if she hadn't felt all of the fifty-six emotions that the stranger described in minutest detail, then certainly she had felt many of them, *enough* of them. Their mutual empathy was immediately sealed.

As she took off her *non*-urethane, *non*-carbon electron free-radical released fair-trade cotton vegan sandals in her yoga studio, and slipped off her hemp fiber compression socks, she felt a sensation of excitement in *some* of her inflamed metatarsophalangeal joints as they met the open air by way of the stranger's scalpel. They both shared a giggle that lasted about seven seconds. As soon as the "giggling" ended, she watched as the stranger set up a toddler-sized microscope and straddled it *whole body*; she sensed the glow of the instrument's 200-watt mercury bulb light up the stranger's bulging right eyeball.

The sensation of having been dissected was odd at first, but surprisingly pleasing, like the high of a jasmine-raspberry tea coming on as a wide-turning city bus nearly crushes you. The stranger then shifted her focus to a left calf hematoma just beginning to surface, and then back to the inflamed metatarsophalangeal joints; additional murmurations on lower limb morbidities worked their way from smooth descriptions of lactic acid hyper-production, to the wrinkled, tubular, curving counters of the newest pharmaceutical speculations about cerebral cortex functions; then something about the bony ridge that ran alongside the lime-encrusted skull of a human ancestor, then back to the four pudgy toes of a nearly extinct ape snuggled next to an imperially imposing distant cousin's fully-flexed pinky. Gradually, she felt a mixture of new emotions escape from her inflamed metatarsophalangeal joints journeying throughout her entire body.

Ever since that fortuitous mid-town Manhattan day, she's had the ability to synchronize her eyes onto others' eyes whose sole focus is—that *thing*. It is a damage/repair understanding of the world. It is also a *life-injecting* exchange between two random people in the big city.

LOS MANIFESTANTES

When their Greek friend announces that he's coming into Denver for the weekend, they both enjoy planning for it over dinner on Friday night. As usual, on the agenda will be an improvised paint-ball gun war in the new hip downtown area by the museum, a late brunch, a one o'clock storefront window shattering spree, bike riding around Cherry Creek Reservoir before sundown, and then, their favorite, lighting police cars on fire while podcasting the live images set to repurposed soccer anthems.

Ball bearings is something they've loved since elementary school, and having experimented with all types and sizes (first chrome steel, then ceramic, then hybrids—20 mm, 40 mm, 80 mm), they know well what they're capable of producing.

They start off by pelting to a pulp the bell-shaped dome of the State Capital, the Greek friend hollering trajectory coordinates, deeply taking in the unfolding glorious image, wiping gold flecks off his goggles, till the round brass cap tumbles to the ground. Quickly, but carefully, they gather several trash bags of government-issued corporate charter deeds and flee the scene. As the Greek friend wonders for a minute just how far his two American friends are willing to go (usually, they make it at least past the brunch, and increasingly, lately, at least till the bike ride around Cherry Creek Reservoir), he unclasps the belt snaps of his olive green canvas bag and entreats his friends to have a quick look inside. As the propylene blast torch comes out of the bag, he adroitly glides the white safety tab so that the red ignition button is exposed, and pressed.

Eventually, after the three have swapped the screaming flame for several rounds (each time the pyre rising higher) and as they move in on the charred corporate charters to add a stream of revolutionary uric acid to the conflagration, the little party comes to an end.

Their black vinyl bibbed Vespas are then unceremoniously dumped into an underground sewer near Cheesman Park. It never becomes a topic of conversation between them as to where the exact location is, nor as to who *exactly* tipped them off to it. It happens as it happens.

The sense of unity and oneness they get from these weekends is something that glues together their diffracted sense of where the world is going for months afterward.

LA ENTIDAD

"Dearest,

I meant to write you last Sunday, but I've been busy with an end-less series of meetings, and a long string of glad-handing dinners. I'll try and do better. I know you've been on pins and needles with anticipation.

Here it is! This pic should give you some idea as to the sort of character I've been 'chaperoning' since I've been here in Area 51, Nevada. Though 'it' is a fair conversationalist (at least through the endolinguo-ombular trumptrometer), and seems fairly well adjusted for its kind, the main thing we 'do' are things that—well, can only be done in the absolute privacy of our still-unacknowl-edged national security silos (I am still, mind you, the *unofficial* ambassador to any and all entities encountered beyond the Kuiper Asteroid Belt).

It actually has (or had) another 'colleague' here in Area 51, a *hype-rio extortio homotron* from the not too distant orange star, Epsi-lon Eridani, who doubles as a 'star student' at the McConough School for International Business at Georgetown University; and that entity (not entirely silicon-based, but *dependent,* for sure) seems completely unaware of my 'guy's' after-hours exploits. For example, the *liquefaction* of 'minor silicon-based life forms' (our agency's designation, actually) for snack food. That's its business I feel.

Look closely at it, that's the exact look it gives me during agency meals in the evening (it's even insinuated itself as a 'senior intern' for the immediate staff around me). When it lightly brushes its globlagular sack with its fingerlets (all sixty), and its gastro-epithelial foam slathers the bottom of its dodeca-labular shelving, it's letting me know that it is (as it calls it) 'cooking.' Today—in addition, it seems to have taken a liking to cornbread, flank steak, and red wine.

When it arrives at my suite, and says 'um . . . I'm ready,' a chill comes over me that's hard to explain. The first time I saw a half-living 'star student' from Georgetown peek out and hide again into its eight-tongued mouth, I was so fascinated, my breath quickened. It felt so *off the record,* so forbidden. When it lowered its globlagular sack onto its blogrornian flap, and let loose 'the colleague' onto my carpet, it seemed to go on forever. It stayed there, 'smiling' (if one could call it that) until the last few clumps of the prospective 'off-shore labor specialist' dropped out of it. What a mess! And I thought, what now?

It immediately took on a Fred Astaire lightness in its motions, scooped up the mess, and flapped it onto my face. I passionately debated about the necessity of such an act, completely smothered in the stuff. The entity's rapturous enthusiasm—if it had been a micron less—might have rendered the night into something utterly unredeemable for me. Instead (and I've been dying to tell you), it was a deeply, non-regulatory, non big-governmental oversight experience—laissez faire at its best. We then debated the ins and outs of various carpet cleaning solutions in that suite for what seemed like a whole week.

It looks forward to meeting you, and has expressed an openness to having you preview its 'Impressions of Nevada' which will be published in The Loose Rocket Review this spring—or maybe even to having you participate in a live poly-lingual version of it in Vegas!

Please kiss our sweet little offspring as you tuck her into bed tonight,

Your loving, tired, 'ambassadorial' Earth mate."

LAS HERMANAS

"We never talk about words in any way, you know, all that linguistics 'signifier-to-signified' jargon completely passed us by. But I've certainly gotten past the hump in terms of thinking of her (the word 'word', my sister) as a fully meaningful/meaning-making being in the world.

This is the—what, 63rd time she's agreed to perform with me in a poetic prose piece. And she does it gladly. Word gets off on the fact of it being kind of off-the-wall (hehe, plus she always ropes in other words for our performances and then casts a reflective-sparkly net of meaning out onto an eternal audience, which is, of course, *not* that—*as* that).

Her curvy typographic shape and oral-muscular articulative requirements, 'w o r d,' I'm sure keeps writers of all kinds constantly on edge (notice that we have a similar, whachamacallit, 'rich in nerves region of significance'). When I first encountered this particular piece, I couldn't help but think of all of the sicko 'journalistic' functions she's been taken to and made to dress up (that too, yes, I've known that for some time now, 'dress up;' there's an unmistakable phonemic sound shift she makes when performing in those places; afterward she's prone to sneaking off with several dozen other genres pretty easily).

She'll eventually settle down, of that I am sure. Word has a conservative streak even. Sometimes I think more than me. I'm sure she'll someday make a great lynchpin to a final argument for the 'humanizing force that is literature.'

Anyway, my mom and dad ('Intuition' and Mr. 'Facts Not Words' (fuck him)) would surely keel over if they knew about these indiscrete applications of herself, this genre hopping. I'm sending this poetic prose piece to you because I know you'll really perv out on it, especially given that she's your *actual living, daily practice.* You sick perv! I can't believe I gave into your demands (me! her twin sister, Gesture). But I love it when you're like this, a completely twisted, totally wicked, pre-linguistic theory of something or other.

The only thing I ask is that you *not* get off too much to this particular piece. Instead, challenge Word, and challenge her good, *super* good. And please save some of that *ineffability* for me, because when I get back (I'm actually working for Reality TV now, sweets), I want you to *de-codify* me—especially in the nether regions of 'performance poetics.'"

LA INVESTIGADORA

By age 6, she could recite entire *Nova Science Channel* transcripts by memory; by 8, she was perfectly fluent in Southern Ohio Appalachian English as well as Michoacán (central Mexican) Spanish as her second and third languages; by 10, her mathematical abilities were so advanced that only a senior year student from Cincinnati Technical College qualified as her private tutor; by 12, her prose style was highly regarded by the Miami University, Ohio, Journalism Department.

At 14, her friend (a shop floor leader at the D-Max diesel engine plant in Moraine, Ohio) introduced her to salvia smoking over a conversation about Industrial Workflow Methods at his family's summer lake cabin just east of Akron. Over the course of that year, her interest in the herb deepened to the point where she studied genetic salvia strains with the goal of synthesizing an entirely new species, while overhauling D-Max's Health, Safety, and the Environment program.

From 15 to 18, employing the tubular ceramic bowl that she designed based on precise calculations of air pressure in each sub-chamber, she smoked at least one thimbleful of salvia in the morning, two at noon, and at least three (sometimes up to five) in the evening. The effect it was having on her overall thinking abilities was something she also studied (and published).

At 19, she—from one day to the next—decided to stop smoking salvia. She also made a decision not to pursue a career in Industrial Workflow Methods. Her new interest was her own complex socio-cultural subjectivity.

By 20, she concluded that the amount of empirical data she gathered from her earlier salvia studies was insufficient to strike out on any definitive path. Her volumes of diagrams, calculations, graphs, charts, and formulas were put into boxes for storage.

At 21, she decided to collect all the necessary data, starting from age 21 to year 24, committing herself to personally acting out every identified form of crosscultural interaction (2,451) in her immediate cultural landscape.

At 25, having completed her colossal temporal-physical regimen which took her to all eighty-eight counties of Ohio, she wrote and published her *Forsensae Temporalis et Carnalis Ohioensis* in Mid-Southern Afro-American English (which she had become enamored with on several of her assignments).

The acknowledgements page to the five-volume collection lists 362 names (in 6 pt. font). The glossary includes over 400 new words for specific types of cross-economic class "dating" interactions alone.

Since then, she's decided to open a coffeehouse in Cleveland's historic warehouse district, making her own pastries, and maybe, maybe, brewing her own beer for the evening happy hour.

EL TERAPISTA

When he agreed to participate in a radical new experiment being conducted in Latvia he had no idea that the results would cause such havoc in his life.

So absolutely perfect, so utterly to spec did his two skull horns turn out, that he spent hours every day gazing at them and feeling them over. Sometimes he would even cancel an entire day's work to be with them alone.

This "relationship" became so crazily demanding that he would spend entire weekends alone by himself. The place he most desired to be was in front of a large mirror. Dressing rooms in unpopular secondhand thrift stores became his favorite place to be.

This condition began to disturb him more and more. He searched for solutions online. Almost all of them required consulting with a professional of some sort. This would be somewhat awkward in that he had just started his own psychotherapeutic practice six months before. He decided to give it some deeper thought when he was less agitated.

As he got to the quiet park along the Hudson River, he slipped off his yellow Tour de France bicycling cap. He hadn't realized how revealing the two protruding lumps of mesh atop his head had become to passers-by. As he sat gazing on the midday sun's rays streaking the tame waters, making him squint, he was suddenly stunned by the Unicorn sitting in the driver's seat of a New York Department of Sanitation green truck.

The strange and difficult-to-piece-together journey from that moment to the moment the standard white, big-eyed Unicorn was spotted passively studying his two horns, is something he's since been trying to render into words in his journal. It's not the species differential that disturbs him the most (despite the mere handful of eons that spanned between his and the Unicorn's common ancestor), nor the twenty superimposed color variations of the truck & driver that made the iris of his eyeballs twirl like umbrellas in the night of a detonated Malaysian nightclub, nor the hard-to-face fact that he did indeed spring up and give chase to the unicorn with the intention of breaking off his horn—grinding it into powder form—mixing it with yeast and guar gum—to make pills—and push them—to kids in his Upper East Side high-rise, what *does* disturb him—deeply, is finding out that his two horns are not really his (in a strict biological sense), but that they're transplants: the horns of a palm reader! From the Bronx! Who accidentally killed himself by a lethal dose of calcium, flax oil, and vitamin E.

His patients know him as a reserved and inquisitive person who asks the right questions at the right time. The specialty listed in his professional profile is "self-esteem theory and its applications."

LA IDEALISTA

Growing up on a remote, sparsely populated underwater complex off the state of Florida, she never had to worry much about mainland-sanctioned codes of "professionalism." She's perfectly comfortable riding her Research Transport Vehicle (RTV) wearing a regular summer surfing wetsuit and a simple corn-based plastic snorkeling mask.

Her day begins with a 5-kilometer, single-passenger, RTV sub ride to the easternmost part of the complex. Once there, in an outcropping of coral where anemone wave in sultry rhythms to the Atlantic's currents, she changes into her two preferred articles of clothing and takes a vigorous 400-meter horizontal dive into the bluish-green waters to collect dying coral samples from a colony slathered in medium-grade sweet crude.

Afterward, in the temperature-controlled sub's cockpit, she eats her packed lunch of cured buffalo-beef cubes garnished with parsley while watching tiger sharks feast on young (or wounded) porpoises. Once she digests, which usually coincides with her skin drying off in the snug cockpit, she slips on the complex-issued, full-body, white nylon lab-wear and speeds back to the western side of the complex.

By now, the hot noon sun has brought to surface a film of red plankton over 500 kilometers in circumference; especially meal-worthy is the pool of flying fish between two packs of orcas. That fish's primordial wings are at least twice as flight-adaptive as any ecotourist's *ideal* of "which way up for Earth?" as they to stumble into the ecocomplex—her home grounds. The same goes for her arms, back, and frontal core musculature—adaptive.

Pineapple juice is what's mainly on her mind as she cruises into the last security sub-station before entering the small village (named "camp veritas") of about two-dozen eco-marine researchers. As soon as she's done gulping down the last few ounces of the cold drink, she steps into a decontaminator (made of a complex ceramic grain-based compound).

By the light of a 900-meter long tube of beamed-in sunlight shin-ing through the hexadecagonally-structured capsule, she slips off her institutional garments before showering her entire body with the decontamination soap (made of a complex aluminum-powered glycerin-based grease). She then inspects the inner lining of the white vinyl wear with her nose. Once the slightly toxic odor has had the full analysis-stimulating effect that she's after, she dabs the noxious moisture from it with her swabs, and detects a sulphurous & ammoniac taste in her upper palate.

From her belt-strapped portable lab kit, she then takes out a long nickel-plated hypodermic and rubs the tip of it in the swab. While peering out from the oval window of the decon capsule, observing colleagues prepare chemical detection slides of their latest samples, watching their children splashing in the indoor marine wonderland-themed pool, and glancing at two somewhat disoriented landfolk taking orders for ice cream treats from the cafeteria manager (her chum from childhood, whom she adores, but just as a friend), she then flush-tests the needle two times before inserting the shiny wand into her left nostril until it bumps into her adenoids. She's learned to enjoy the slight pain that radiates from hitting that spot.

Later in the day, after verifying her "toxin-free" status, she leads a heated discussion about "needed policy shifts" at the main lab's meeting room (the ceiling beams are made from simple algae-based polymer fibers). As her well-targeted words dissipate into the artificially pumped-in air ducts, she unclasps the small silver chain amulet around her neck, opens its tiny chamber, and releases a small gust of freshly aerated lorazepam onto her colleagues' faces.

LAS GLOBALISTAS

From rural Maryland to an old castle in Luxembourg—she can hardly believe she's actually here, acting in her first movie, as an extra, working on a "twenty American media promo whizz kids punk-slapped (one by one)" *scene* with the illustrious French star of the movie.

The director decided to keep the film crew at a minimum so the two could find the mental space to completely settle into the sequence. So, for now, the only ones present were the director (a Russian man—of 17), the camera (a Korean girl—of 62), the lighting tech (an Argentinean guy—in transition—of 44) and the two actresses (21 and 25, American and French, respectively).

By the sixth or seventh shoot, they were not acting anymore, aggression-induced saliva was frothing from their mouths, their noses were dripping blood, their fingers were smeared with blood, saliva, and tears. The darkness of the small castle chapel echoed with the sounds of face cheeks snapping and teeth splattering against the mold-coated, stone walls.

Then, rather suddenly, a kind of Global Pop Culture fuzzy feeling started to come over the both of them. Fingers were now being re-directed into their *own* noses. At times, singular, firm slaps were laid across their *own* faces, making the room resound with the fury of their newly discovered chronic inner boredom. By the end of the twelfth take, faces had been patched up enough so as to rec-ognize who was who; as they sat side by side at the black-lacquered wooden alter, they spoke as if possessed by their respective "places of origin."

The camera (but not the light above it) had actually been switched off after the twelfth shoot, though the actresses didn't know it at the time. The director looked at the camera girl, and in a wink of mutual agreement, they allowed the two actresses to delve deeper into this two-person global-professional fizzle-fest.

By now, they both had managed to blurt out some specific require-ments of their respective "national sensibilities," and were desper-ately trying to recoup a single personal-national memory worthy of translating into *any* language known to humankind. The light was then turned off. It was pitch dark, and slowly the sound of their excited murmuring quieted. After five minutes, the strange silence prompted the lighting tech to turn the light back on.

The American was dancing in a sort of one-person square dance, her mouth gaping open, her hands occasionally gripping the secu-rity of the black-lacquered wooden alter (though she actually broke off a sizeable chunk of it). A steady trickle of sweat was leaking from her forehead down to her clavicles. The French girl's neck muscles were bulging as she pushed against the mold-covered stone wall with the top of her head. Suddenly, a little squeak came out of the American, a squeak that blended horror with pleasure. The French girl then gradually stopped pushing her head against the wall and, while facing the American, performed a barely-perceptible one-person minuet—for about a minute.

After the shoot, in the brightly lit bathroom (former dungeon), they both cleaned themselves of any castle *gunk* (as well as any stray DNA) with wet towels. The American, while drying herself off, paused briefly and looked at the other girl with a blank look, and in a quiet, hoarse tone said, "thanks for that," and then broke into a soft smile. The French actress put her index finger on the American's nose and (in an even quieter tone) said, "fuck you."

LOS COLABORADORES

They let go of their last line of defense. A warm, tingly calm washes over their bodies. This, for now, is the activity they really want to sink into on a patch of soft grass.

Sometimes life is that simple. Sometimes all of the deflected desires, pyschosocial subterfuge, private intrigues, and deep-seated anxieties of trying to understand the complex world they live in gives way to the pleasures of reshuffling those stresses when thumbing through a new nerdy book of poetry on a cool Sunday afternoon in July.

LA OBSERVADORA

Feeling the initial jolts of an explosive, subterranean social trans-formation is something that she lives for, especially when the jolts are perceived to erupt from nearly frozen bystanders' warm, pul-sating bodies.

First, their emotions brighten to a maximum luminosity, spectacu-lar accidents in thought causing intention to splinter into multiple paths of action; next, their ideals deflate and tuck hard against actual lived conditions; after that, their sense of public vanity dissipates, a scattering plume of smoke to nowhere; finally, their dogged dedication to reason clamps its straining claws into a rapidly unfolding speculative science of a just-around-the-corner "reality."

The jolts come in a series of flickering dream images, sending waves of recovered historical memory into her sense of The Now.

She adores this new "little demon" friend more than anything else in the world. The feeling is mutual.

EL REFUGIADO

Southeast California, the midday temperature has reached 105. The month-long guest strolls out half naked onto the ranch motel's porch. The quiet, conservative owner immediately detects the morally unanchored sass in the guest's attitude. The guest (as he has every single day) *over-rocks* the rocking chair as his chrome flask of rye whisky finds its way to his impudent, Brooklyn-based mouth.

Two hours later, after the inn keeper's canine has completed its usual solo attack raid on room 7, the guest recommits to confronting his toiled-over "writer ready" texts, looking to "flip" them (hard) into "reader ready" fables, squeezing a few last drops of transpersonal nectar onto each of them.

Later, in the evening, the guest texts his consigliere in Elisaville, New York: "surveillance here / *pazzo* watching / no matter / *pazzo* poetized / words flowing / still risky / can stay / want to / no car / send booze / send beans / quality soap! / the title? / still pondering / proprietor asleep! / clouds clearing / stars glowing / sage pungent / butterflies aloft / what's real / what's not / tipping point / cross point / point of no return / horizon appears / *so far* / so near."